Patricia Ryan Nixon

Patricia Ryan Nixon

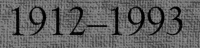

1912–1993

BY BARBARA SILBERDICK FEINBERG

CHILDREN'S PRESS®
A Division of Grolier Publishing
New York London Hong Kong Sydney
Danbury, Connecticut

Consultant: LINDA CORNWELL
                   Learning Resource Consultant
                   Indiana Department of Education

Project Editor: DOWNING PUBLISHING SERVICES
Page Layout: CAROLE DESNOES
Photo Researcher: JAN IZZO

Visit Children's Press on the Internet at:
http://publishing.grolier.com

Library of Congress Cataloging-in-Publication Data
Feinberg, Barbara Silberdick.
        Patricia Ryan Nixon / by Barbara Silberdick Feinberg.
              p. cm. — (Encyclopedia of first ladies)
        Includes bibliographical references and index.
        Summary: A biography of an intensely private person remembered for her many
achievements as First Lady and admired for loyalty to her husband, the thirty-
seventh president of the United States.
        ISBN 0-516-20482-3
        1. Nixon, Pat, 1912–1993—Juvenile literature.   2. Presidents' spouses—United
States—Biography—Juvenile literature.   3. Nixon, Richard M. (Richard
Milhous), 1913–1994—Juvenile literature. [1. Nixon, Pat, 1912–1993.   2. First
ladies. 3. Women—Biography.]   I. Title. II. Series.
E857.N58F45   1998
973.924'092—dc21   98-21382
[B]   CIP
                                                                 AC

Table of Contents

Patricia Ryan Nixon

CHAPTER ONE

A Devoted Daughter

✳ ✳ ✳ ✳ ✳ ✳ ✳ ✳ ✳ ✳ ✳ ✳ ✳ ✳ ✳ ✳ ✳

Thelma Catherine Ryan was born on March 16, 1912—St. Patrick's Day Eve. When her father, William Ryan, returned home from work around midnight, he welcomed his "St. Patrick's Day babe in the morn" and nicknamed her Pat. As a proud Irish-American, he even insisted that her birthday be celebrated on March 17. His wife reluctantly agreed.

In 1909, Will, an unsuccessful prospector, had met and married Kate Halberstadt Bender in South Dakota. She was a widow with two young children, Matthew and Neva. The family soon moved to Ely, Nevada, a rich source of precious metals. Will became

✳ ✳ ✳ ✳ ✳ ✳ ✳ ✳ ✳ ✳ ✳ ✳ ✳ ✳ ✳ ✳ ✳

Portrait of America, 1912: Modern America Takes Shape

☆ ☆ ☆ ☆ ☆ ☆ ☆ ☆ ☆ ☆ ☆ ☆ ☆ ☆ ☆ ☆ ☆ ☆ ☆ ☆

In 1912, the year Pat Ryan was born, New Mexico and Arizona joined the Union. Now, all the land in the continental United States, from the Atlantic to the Pacific, was divided into states. America took its modern shape.

Like Pat's family, more than half of the country's 92.5 million people still lived in rural areas. But America's future seemed to be in the cities. Huge corporations there provided jobs for thousands of workers. Factories needed laborers; offices hired record numbers of secretaries. Soon, more Americans would live and work in the cities than anywhere else. From the hustle and bustle emerged a new middle class of people. They lived comfortably and were neither wealthy nor poor. Many of them were angry at the social conditions they saw around them. Called Progressives, they worked for social justice and reform. African Americans still suffered terribly. Their lives had grown worse since Reconstruction. Most lived in the rural South under dismal conditions. Violence against them increased. Laws segregated black people from white society and made it difficult for them to vote.

America's new middle class, meanwhile, had time to enjoy life. They took vacations in their Model T Fords and flocked to baseball games. (Boston beat New York in the 1912 World Series.) More than 10 million Americans attended the movies each week. In a small town called Hollywood, the brand-new movie industry produced hundreds of short comedies to satisfy them. Americans loved dancing, too, especially to fast music. Young women jiggled and swayed to the Turkey Trot and the Bunny Hop, ignoring the disapproval of their elders. Poetry, literature, and art flourished. Artists began to experiment with new styles. Painters used bold colors and abstract patterns to capture the energy of urban life.

A month after Pat's birth, the sinking of the luxury liner *Titanic* shocked the world. On its first voyage, the most modern, largest, and fastest steamship ever built struck an iceberg and went down with 1,500 people. The ship was traveling too fast in dangerous waters. Many people wondered if the modern world was, too.

Pat's mother, Kate Halberstadt Bender, married William Ryan in 1909.

Pat, her brothers, and her father posed for this picture outside their home in Artesia, California.

a mining engineer. Keeping house in a canvas tent, Kate gave birth to William, Jr., in 1909, and Thomas in 1910, before Pat was born.

When Pat was a year old, the Ryans traveled to Artesia, now Cerritos, California, 20 miles (32 kilometers) outside Los Angeles. They bought 10 acres (4 hectares) of land to farm in this rural community. Pat grew up in a five-room house that had no electric lighting, no indoor bathroom, and no running water for the kitchen sink. It was a hard life. Like most farm children, Pat did her share of chores. "I worked right along with my brothers in the fields, really, which was lots of fun. We picked potatoes; we picked tomatoes; we picked peppers and cauliflower. When I was real tiny, I just tagged along. But when I got older, I drove the team of horses." Her brothers were her constant companions at home and at school.

Nevada, U.S.A.

✫ ✫

When we think of Nevada today, we think of the lights and excitement of Las Vegas. However, that city represents only a small corner of the state. Nevada is mostly rugged and dry. It was called *Nevada*, a Spanish word meaning "snow-capped," because miles of snow-covered mountain ranges rise from its hot deserts. The population is small and spread out. Even the state symbols are hardy: sage-brush (state flower), desert bighorn sheep (state animal), sandstone (state rock), and desert tortoise (state reptile). When Pat Ryan was born there in 1912, there was no Las Vegas, but people came to Nevada in search of other riches. Since 1859, the discovery of gold and silver in Nevada's mountains had lured miners and fortune hunters. Towns sprang up in the wilderness where men pulled precious metals from the earth. The Comstock Lode, the richest of all the finds, has yielded $900 million in minerals over the years. After 1900, prospectors rushed to Ely, Pat's birthplace, to mine the bountiful copper deposits discovered there.

From 1909 to 1913, the Ryans lived in the small, dusty town of Ely, Nevada, where Pat's father worked as a mining engineer.

Pat Ryan's childhood home in what is now Cerritos, California, has been restored and is now the centerpiece of Pat Nixon Park, which also includes a children's playground.

The Ryan's home in the rural community of Artesia was located only a few miles from the bustling city of Los Angeles, shown here as it looked in 1910.

Oranges, Oil, and Opportunity

☆ ☆

The hometown of Pat's youth is today a part of the vast metropolis of greater Los Angeles. When she was a girl, however, southern California bloomed with citrus groves and bristled with oil wells. In 1913, a huge aqueduct (a system for transporting water) was built to provide the dry land with water from the Owens Valley 250 miles (402 km) to the north. More and more people flocked to the region, which had gained a reputation as an American paradise. Early moviemakers, who had been working in New York City and Chicago, discovered that the year-round warm climate and bright sunshine of southern California made filming easier. Nearly overnight, the quiet town of Hollywood, about 20 miles (32 km) north of Artesia, was turned into the capital of American filmmaking.

Since Pat was seven years younger than her half-sister Neva, the two had little in common.

Pat's earliest memories were of outings away from the farm. She recalled waiting in the wagon while her father bought supplies in town. "I'd watch the corner to see if he came back carrying a strawberry ice-cream cone. That would be a big treat." Quite often, there wasn't enough money to buy ice cream. Pat also enjoyed trolley-car rides with her mother to visit her half-brother Matthew in Los Angeles. He was being raised by his father's parents, who could give him more advantages than the Ryans could. Pat did not get to know him well.

As she was growing up, Pat loved to listen to her father's stories about his family and his adventures. He had been a deckhand on a whaling ship, a surveyor in the Philippines, measuring land; and a miner seeking his fortune in the Alaska gold rush of 1898.

Her mother's family history was a mystery to Pat. Born into a farming

Pat loved listening to her father's stories about his many adventures, including the time he spent as a deckhand on a whaling ship like these.

Pat's adventurous father joined prospectors like these during the Alaska gold rush of 1898.

family in Germany, Kate came to the United States at the age of ten. Kate was afraid to tell her children about her past because of mounting anti-German feelings. The United States entered World War I in 1917, fighting alongside Britain and France against Germany and Austria. This prompted some Americans to destroy shops belonging to German-Americans and ban all things German, from music to frankfurters and sauerkraut. A fearful Kate made her children promise not to tell anyone that their mother was a German immigrant.

When Pat turned six, she went to grammar school, walking $1\frac{1}{4}$ miles (2 km) each way. Only her teachers knew her as Thelma. Her friends called her "Buddy," and to her brothers, she was "Babe."

Pat was a good student and skipped

World War I: Fast Facts

WHAT: The "Great War," the "War to End All Wars," the first truly global conflict

WHEN: 1914–1918

WHO: The Central European Powers, including Austria-Hungary and Germany, opposed the Allied Powers, including Britain, France, and Russia. The United States entered the war on the Allied side in 1917.

WHERE: The Central Powers invaded Serbia, Romania, Russia, Belgium, France, and Italy. Fighting extended into the Atlantic Ocean and the Mediterranean Sea.

WHY: European disputes over land, economics, religion, and leadership boiled over in 1914 when Austrian archduke Francis Ferdinand was assassinated on a visit to Serbia. Austria declared war on Serbia, and other European nations picked sides. The United States got involved largely because German submarine warfare disrupted commerce in the North Atlantic Ocean.

OUTCOME: The Central Powers fell to the Allied Powers in 1918, and a peace treaty was signed on November 11. The map of Europe was redrawn and the League of Nations was founded to settle international disputes. Ten million soldiers, including 116,500 Americans, had died.

Pat kept up her grades at Excelsior High School (left) while she ran the Ryan household and did farm chores.

grades. She soon caught up with Bill and Tom. Pat was always a tomboy, preferring active games to dolls and playing house. After school, she and her friends raided nearby beehives, walked on railroad tracks across a bridge, and climbed a two-story water tank that served as a stage for their plays. Alone, she would hoist herself into her brothers' tree house to read books. She felt that reading "gave me a horizon beyond the small town we were living in. Somehow I always knew there was more in the world than we were experiencing then."

The Ryan children quickly learned to hide their feelings since Will did not encourage displays of affection or anger. When he occasionally drank too much, his temper would flare up, and he would pick fights with his wife. Her father's outbursts left their mark on Pat. "I detest temper. I detest scenes. I just can't be that way. I saw it with my father . . . and so to avoid scenes or unhappiness, I suppose I [gave in] to others."

During the summer of 1925, when she was thirteen, Pat proved how strong she could be. Her half-sister Neva had received some money from her grandparents and moved out of the Ryan household to attend a junior college. Soon after she left, Kate became too sick to take care of the family. Pat took over her mother's responsibilities, and her brothers did what they could to help. She did not tell any of her friends that Kate was dying of cancer and kidney disease. During the last weeks of her mother's life, Pat often nursed Kate at night, feeding her and keeping her tidy. Kate died on January 18, 1926. After the funeral service, Pat tried to put everyone at ease. She kept her grief to herself.

While running the household and doing farm chores, Pat kept up her grades at Excelsior High School. She

Even though she had many responsibilities, Pat (center) found some time for fun.

Pat (seated, fourth from left) was vice president of the Excelsior High School drama club, Les Marionettes.

These pictures of (left to right) William, Pat (Thelma), and Tom Ryan appeared in the Excelsior High School yearbook.

often studied for tests while ironing her brothers' shirts. She still managed to find time for fun, but the pretty auburn-haired girl with hazel eyes was allowed to date only if her brothers were part of the group. Pat was elected secretary of the student government and was an active member of the debate and drama clubs. Appearing in school plays offered her a chance to feel glamorous and to escape from her burdens. To her classmates and teachers, she was capable and calm.

Shortly before her senior year began, Pat had learned that her father was dying of a lung disease. She informed Will's family back East, and her aunt Annie Rockwell arrived in January to visit for a few weeks. In June 1929, the three young Ryans graduated with college scholarships, but there wasn't enough money for all of them to leave home, and Will needed care. They decided that Tom would attend the University of Southern California (USC) in Los Angeles while Bill managed the farm and Pat nursed their father. Later that summer, Will moved to a sanatorium, a special hospital for patients with lung diseases. Pat took a job at the bank to pay for his care and drove an hour each way to see him whenever she could. He died on May 5, 1930, and was buried next to his wife. In 1931, Will's devoted daughter changed her name to Patricia, his favorite name.

Working the farm no longer brought in enough cash to support the Ryans. They rented out the land and received just enough money to pay their taxes. Like many Americans, they were feeling the effects of the Great Depression. The nation's economy had ground to a halt, with businesses and factories closing. Almost 13 million Americans were jobless. Bill joined Tom in Los Angeles. Pat remained alone in Artesia. She attended Fullerton Junior College while working as a janitor and bookkeeper at the local bank to support herself. When she lost the jobs, she decided to follow her father's example and travel. She had become an independent woman.

CHAPTER TWO

An Independent Woman

☆ ☆ ☆ ☆ ☆ ☆ ☆ ☆ ☆ ☆ ☆ ☆ ☆ ☆ ☆ ☆ ☆ ☆

"I always wanted to do something else besides be buried in a small town," Pat stated. That is why she jumped at the chance to drive an elderly couple from California to Connecticut in exchange for bus fare home. Despite the failure of the car's cooling system in the Arizona desert, numerous flat tires, and brake problems in the mountains, the three finally arrived in the East. Pat was reunited with her aunt Annie and met her other Ryan relatives.

With help from her aunt Kate, a nun, Pat got a secretarial job at Old Seton Hospital, in New York City. The hospital treated patients with fatal lung diseases.

☆ ☆ ☆ ☆ ☆ ☆ ☆ ☆ ☆ ☆ ☆ ☆ ☆ ☆ ☆ ☆ ☆ ☆

During the two years she worked at Old Seton Hospital in New York City, Pat (center) spent many weekends in Ridgefield, Connecticut, with her cousins Alice (left) and Josephine Rockwell (right).

Pat's aunt headed the X-ray department and pharmacy. After a summer course at Columbia University, Pat qualified to operate X-ray equipment. She was very moved by the many young patients who wanted so desperately to live. She wrote to her brother Bill, "Sometimes I feel that I should like to spend my life just working for the afflicted unfortunates [the very ill] —helping them to be more happy." At times, Pat broke hospital rules by sneaking out to go sledding with patients.

Coast-to-Coast Contrast

✦ ✦

When Pat Ryan made that drive across the country from Los Angeles to New York, she traveled 3,000 miles (4,828 km) and a world away. The island of Manhattan must have seemed tall, dark, and crowded to the California girl. The Empire State Building, then the world's tallest, had just been completed in 1931. Other skyscrapers turned the streets into blustery canyons where little sunshine could reach. People traveled underground over hundreds of miles of subway line. With nearly 7 million people, the city was an international center of business, art, theater, and music. Los Angeles was, by contrast, a sprawling, centerless city that spread out over hundreds of square miles. Southern sun and mild Pacific breezes washed over its low buildings and open landscape. Although its population was growing rapidly, fewer than 1.5 million people lived in Los Angeles in the 1930s. Compared to bustling New York City, early LA seemed like a relaxed small town.

Pat worked on student research programs at USC, along with a variety of other jobs, to help pay her tuition. The Los Angeles Times ran this picture of Pat (on the left) and a fellow student as they stuffed a mailbag with questionnaires that would be sent to former students.

A doctor at the hospital wanted to marry her, but Pat had other plans for her future. Unlike most young women her age, she was not yet ready to settle down. She decided to return to California and get her college degree.

In the fall of 1934, she moved into her brothers' cramped bungalow in Los Angeles and enrolled at USC.

Because Pat's university scholarship did not pay all her expenses, she took a variety of jobs. She worked as an extra in the movies, earning $7 a day. She got walk-on parts in *Becky Sharp, The Great Ziegfeld,* and *Small Town Girl*. She turned down an offer to play a small part in one film, explaining that "it seemed so very boring . . . going over and over and over about three words until you almost went mad." At other times, Pat worked as a dental assistant, a telephone operator, and as a model at a department store. She also held a number of jobs on campus. Professor Frank Baxter noted that she always looked tired when she came to class. He knew why. "As I recall it, if you went into the cafeteria, there was Pat Ryan at the serving counter. An hour later, if you went to the library, there was Pat Ryan checking out books. And if you came back to the campus that evening, there was Pat Ryan working on some student research program."

In 1937, Pat graduated with honors, a teaching certificate, and a degree in merchandising. She took the first job she was offered, teaching typing and shorthand to business students at Whittier Union High School. Her salary was $1,800 a year. One of her former students remembers that "she treated us warmly, but she insisted on results. . . . She allowed no compromises, no errors, no second-rate job." Another described her as "happy, enthusiastic, sprightly." She was popular with students and teachers alike. Because Pat was so energetic and outgoing, students chose her as their faculty adviser to the Pep Committee. The committee organized rallies and half-time activities for football games.

To Pat, Whittier was much like Artesia, just another small farming town outside Los Angeles. While it had only one movie house, it did have an amateur theater group, the Whittier Community Players. In 1938, Pat joined the group and tried out for a small part. Richard M. Nixon, already cast as a prosecutor in the drama, watched her as she read for the role. He wrote, "For me, it was a case of love at first sight." After Pat got the part, Nixon asked a friend to introduce him to her and offered to drive her home. When Pat refused his first request for a date, he told her, "You shouldn't say that, because someday

Richard Nixon's parents, Frank and Hannah, owned a general store in Whittier. Pat sometimes went to the store to help bake pies and cakes for the customers.

I'm going to marry you!" Pat's reaction was decidedly unromantic: "I thought he was nuts or something."

It was two and a half years before the earnest young Whittier lawyer was able to persuade Pat to become his wife. He pursued her with great determination, learning to ice skate to please her, and helping her grade papers. He even drove her to and from Los Angeles when she dated other men. Later, she insisted, "I admired Dick Nixon from the very beginning, but I was having a very good time and wasn't anxious to settle down." In time, she grew fond of him. She even showed up at the Nixon family's grocery store to help his mother Hannah bake pies and cakes for the customers.

Pat accepted Richard's proposal in March 1940. He sent her an engagement ring in a basket of flowers. At

Richard Nixon and Pat Ryan were married on June 21, 1940, at the Mission Inn in Riverside. Pat was twenty-eight, older than most women of her time, when she was finally ready to marry.

The Quakers

*　*　*　*　*　*　*　*　*　*　*　*　*　*　*　*　*　*　*　*

Today's Quaker religion dates back to a movement in seventeenth-century England. Formally called the Society of Friends, Quakers believed that the spirit of God was alive in everyone. They rejected the need for clergy, the violence of war, and the inhumanity of slavery. Punished for their beliefs in England, many Quakers fled to the American colonies to find freedom to practice their religion. To worship, they gathered in "meetings." Because those overcome by the divine spirit might tremble uncontrollably, they earned the name "Quakers." In the twentieth century, Quakers became known for their concern with humanitarian issues and for their excellent schools. Richard Nixon was not the only Quaker president; Herbert Hoover, in office from 1929 to 1933, was also a Quaker. More than 300,000 Quakers live around the world today.

the age of twenty-eight, much later than most women of her time, she was ready to marry. She even adopted Richard's Quaker religion. The couple had a simple wedding ceremony on June 21, 1940, at the Mission Inn in Riverside. They took a two-week trip to Mexico, bringing cans of food with them to save money on meals. Some of the wedding guests stripped the labels from the cans, so the Nixons never knew what each meal would bring. It made eating an adventure.

When they came back to Whittier, Pat resumed her teaching while Richard continued to practice law at a local law firm. After the Japanese bombed Pearl Harbor, Hawaii, on December 7, 1941, the United States entered World War II. It sided with Britain and the Soviet Union against Germany, Italy, and Japan. To support the war effort, the Nixons went to Washington and took jobs with the Office of Price Administration (OPA). This government agency regulated the prices Americans paid for products that were scarce because of

World War II: Fast Facts

WHAT: The second great global conflict

WHEN: 1939–1945

WHO: The Axis Powers, including Germany, Italy, and Japan, opposed the Allies, including Britain, France, and the USSR. The United States entered the war on the Allied side in 1941 after the bombing by Japan of Pearl Harbor in Hawaii.

WHERE: Fighting raged throughout the Pacific Ocean and in the Atlantic Ocean as well as from Scandinavia to North Africa, and deep into the Soviet Union.

WHY: Chancellor Adolf Hitler, setting out to make Germany the most powerful country in the world, began by invading his European neighbors. Japan, Italy, and Germany pledged support to one another in 1940. When the United States declared war on Japan after the attack on Pearl Harbor in 1941, Germany and Italy declared war on the United States.

OUTCOME: The war ended in stages. Germany surrendered in May 1945. Japan surrendered after the United States dropped two atomic bombs there in August. More than 400,000 American troops died in battle; about 17 million on both sides perished.

Richard Nixon as a lieutenant commander in the U. S. Navy during World War II

Richard carried this photo of Pat with him while he was stationed in the South Pacific.

military needs. Since the Quaker religion condemned violence, Richard could have been excused from military service. Nevertheless, in 1942, he enlisted in the navy.

As they moved from one naval base to another, Pat made slipcovers and drapes to decorate the tiny apartments they occupied. Although she took any job she could find, she firmly believed that "a woman must first and foremost be a homemaker." Because of the war, many women were now juggling work and household duties. When Richard shipped off to the Pacific, Pat worked for the OPA in San Francisco. At war's end in 1945, Richard returned, and Pat unexpectedly found herself the wife of a politician.

Women on the Home Front

✭ ✭

With so many American men fighting in Europe and the Pacific during World War II, who stayed home to make the ammunition, ships, and planes? A familiar song from the 1940s can tell you: "Rosie the Riveter." To help the war effort, America's women took on a "double day," working a full shift day or night and caring for home and children the rest of the time. With only a little training, women worked as welders, press operators, and riveters. They did these jobs so well that production levels rose dramatically despite the loss of men to the military. For the first time, women received the high pay of skilled laborers. With the return of the soldiers, however, posters went up urging women to "Give Back Their Jobs" and showing a woman handing over her drill. Opportunities for women in the workplace again grew scarce, and they were encouraged to return to homemaking.

This "Rosie the Riveter" painting by Edna Reindel is called Catship Burner.

CHAPTER THREE

A Politician's Wife

★ ★ ★ ★ ★ ★ ★ ★ ★ ★ ★ ★ ★ ★ ★ ★ ★ ★

"I told him it was his decision, and I would do what he liked," Pat remembered. Richard had turned to her for advice when some California businessmen asked him to run for Congress. Pat was not very interested in politics, but she knew that he wanted a political career. Like many other wartime wives, she was ready to leave the workplace and devote herself to her husband's peacetime needs and interests.

The high cost of campaigning for office troubled her. Richard would have to win a primary election, competing against others to become the Republican party's official candidate. Only then would he receive cam-

★ ★ ★ ★ ★ ★ ★ ★ ★ ★ ★ ★ ★ ★ ★ ★ ★ ★

During his 1946 congressional campaign, Richard Nixon posed with his baby daughter Tricia.

Hannah Nixon, in January 1946. On February 21, Pat gave birth to daughter Patricia, called Tricia. Three weeks later, she left Tricia with grandmother Hannah Nixon. During the day, Pat used her enormous energy and considerable business skills to help her husband win office. At night, she stayed up comforting the wakeful infant so her husband could sleep undisturbed. Pat also did the laundry and kept her husband's navy uniforms looking crisp. She had given away his old clothes to relatives. Due to postwar shortages, it was several months before he was able to get a new suit.

Neither Richard nor Pat had ever campaigned before, but they learned quickly. In their one-room, storefront headquarters, Pat typed campaign materials and answered letters. How frustrated she was when there wasn't enough money to buy postage stamps. She was horrified when a large number of costly printed pamphlets were stolen and destroyed. Occasionally, Pat accompanied Richard when he made speeches and handed out leaflets. She greeted volunteers and thanked them for helping out, but she

paign funds from the party. Like most young married couples, the Nixons had been saving to buy a house. They agreed to use this money, plus several thousand dollars Richard had won playing poker in the navy, to run in the primary.

Because vacant apartments were hard to find, Richard and Pat moved in with his parents, Frank and did not make speeches. The former high-school debater would no longer speak in public. She insisted that only one person should be talking about the issues—her husband. Pat also attended numerous social functions, such as teas and coffee klatches, to win votes for her husband. She did not enjoy campaigning for votes, but she did it for him. As she later explained, "In 1946, not many wives were active in politics. But we were so anxious to win I just thought of ways I could be most helpful."

After his primary victory, Richard took on Representative Jerry Voorhis, a Democrat, who had already won five elections to the House. Nixon was an unknown. That changed when Richard charged that Voorhis's voting record in Congress was sympathetic to communism. (Communism was a set of ideas emphasizing state ownership of the economy in the name of the people, practiced by the former Soviet Union and the states it once controlled.) Pat had done much of the research on Voorhis's voting record for Richard. Some people accused Nixon of unfairly linking Voorhis to commu-

Richard Nixon ran against Representative Jerry Voorhis during the 1946 campaign for Congress.

nism, but Pat never questioned her husband's views or the methods he employed to win office. Of his victory, Richard wrote, "Pat and I were happier on November 6, 1946 [the day after Election Day], than we were ever to be again in my political career."

As a new congressman's wife, Pat had few official duties. Occasionally, she went over the mail at her husband's office. Mostly, she looked after Tricia, kept house, and helped Richard's parents. The elder Nixons

had bought a dairy farm in Pennsylvania and were not in good health. Pat attended meetings of the Congressional Wives Club, a social group, and was caught up in a whirl of dinner parties and receptions. She stretched her limited budget so she would look well-groomed when she appeared at her husband's side. Unfortunately, she saw less and less of

Congressman Richard Nixon in 1947 biking with Pat and Tricia at the Tidal Basin in Washington, D.C.

him. Richard traveled to Europe with a congressional committee and visited his district in California without her. When he decided to run for reelection in 1948, Pat was pregnant with their second child. She admitted to him that she was very unhappy with his decision to run again. He promised to spend more time at home with her, a promise he tried to keep.

On July 5, 1948, Pat gave birth to daughter Julie. Her mother-in-law came to help out, but she became sick. Alone, Pat had to take care of

Hannah, the newborn baby, and two-year-old Tricia. Richard was busy with the upcoming political campaign and the Alger Hiss case. Nixon had accused Hiss, a former State Department employee, of lying about his Communist ties. Hiss denied the charges but was later convicted of lying in court. Pat had to stand by as reporters and cartoonists supporting Hiss ridiculed her husband. She defended him, claiming, "He did what he felt was right."

Trusting the children to babysit-

Red Scares and Black Lists

☆ ☆ ☆ ☆ ☆ ☆ ☆ ☆ ☆ ☆ ☆ ☆ ☆ ☆ ☆ ☆ ☆ ☆ ☆ ☆

After World War II, Americans began to fear the spread of communism because the Soviet Union had taken over many countries. Alger Hiss was a former government employee accused of turning classified U.S. documents over to Soviet agents. Microfilm copies of papers in his handwriting from the Departments of State, Navy, and War were produced as evidence, and he was convicted of lying in his testimony before the House Un-American Activities Committee. The fear of communism, known as the Red Scare, soon got out of hand. A senator named Joseph McCarthy led a vicious crusade against Americans he believed to have communist ties. Some former FBI agents made money by selling lists of the names of people suspected of having anything to do with the Communist party. They were called "blacklists." For many years, blacklisted Americans suffered terribly by losing their jobs or going to jail. Worst of all, the Red Scare discouraged the freedom of thought and expression upon which the United States was founded.

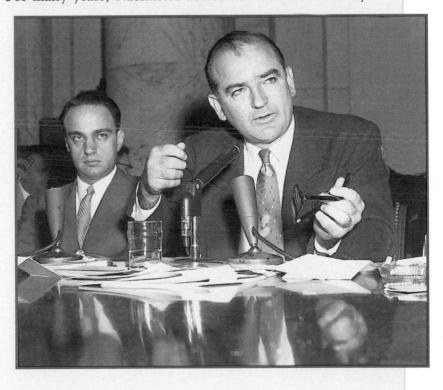

During the Red Scare of the late 1940s and early 1950s, Senator Joseph McCarthy (on the right) accused many Americans of having communist ties.

Congressman Richard Nixon waves from a car during his campaign for the U.S. Senate in 1950.

ters, Pat accompanied Richard all over the state of California when he decided to run for the U.S. Senate in 1950. She managed to look neat and trim, no matter how exhausted she was. Her wardrobe was meager. So several friends in Whittier knitted her three suits, which she wore with pride. Pat grew increasingly disgusted with the bitterly fought campaign. Richard accused his opponent, Democrat Helen Gahagan Douglas, of being pro-communist, calling her the "Pink Lady." She charged him with dirty politics, labeling him "Tricky Dicky."

With Richard's victory, the Nixons at last were able to afford a house in Washington, D.C. Pat supervised the move, looked after the children, and still found time to help out at her hus-

Nixon holds a child during his 1950 Senate campaign against Democrat Helen Gahagan Douglas.

band's office. Pat explained, "I did all the chores so that he could use his energy for the problems at hand." Richard traveled even more, giving speeches and fund-raising for his party.

In 1952, the bright young senator from California was discussed as a candidate for vice president. Seeking a peaceful, quiet family life, Pat was half-hoping he wouldn't accept the post even if it was offered. As a loyal wife, she went with him to Chicago where the nominations for president and vice president were being made.

Helen Gahagan Douglas

Fun Fashions of the Fifties

✶ ✶

By the 1950s, Americans were tired of the conservative clothes of the World War II years. When the national emergency had passed, people shook off their gloom and put on bright colors and flashy styles. New materials that were developed during the war to replace scarce wool and cotton were now used to make modern, easy-to-care-for "wash-and-wear" clothes. Now that shortages of fabric and materials were over, women added volumes of material and layers of petticoats to their skirts. Polka dots and stripes decorated everything from neckties to swimsuits. Men added pink to their drab, gray wardrobes. Some women cropped their hair into a curly mass called a poodle cut. Others teased, pinned, and sprayed their long locks into a towering beehive on top of their heads. Many young men slicked their hair back into "ducktails."

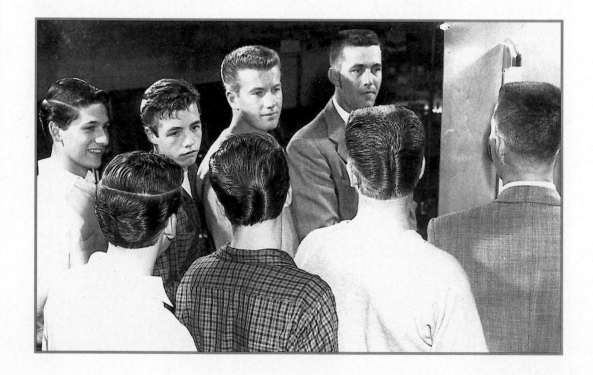

Richard posing at home with Pat and Tricia during the Senate campaign

Republican presidential nominee Dwight Eisenhower stretches his arms in response to an ovation at the Republican National Convention. Among those applauding are Pat Nixon (second from left) and vice-presidential nominee Richard Nixon (center).

Richard and Pat Nixon smile widely on the podium after Richard accepted his nomination as the Republican candidate for vice president.

Dwight D. Eisenhower (1890–1969)

✮ ✮

Dwight "Ike" Eisenhower emerged from the poverty of his Kansas childhood to become one of America's most brilliant, and beloved, military leaders. During World War II, he rose to the top of the Allied command. After planning many of the major battles of the war, he returned a hero. In 1952, the people elected the grandfatherly general the thirty-fourth president of the United States. Even though he had been a soldier, President Eisenhower fondly wished for peace in a world frightened by the threat of nuclear weapons. To wage peace, he would have to fight a different kind of battle called the Cold War. The Cold War amounted to a tense standoff between the United States and the Soviet Union. Each afraid of the other, the two great nations—one democratic and one communist—raced to build bigger and better weapons. Eisenhower knew that a nuclear conflict would mean total destruction. He tried hard to slow the build-up of arms by cutting American defense spending and talking with the Soviet leader. But the Cold War raged on. Eisenhower would not live to see it end, finally, with the breakup of the Soviet Union in 1991.

Pat was sure that Richard would not be offered the nomination. She was eating a sandwich in a restaurant when she learned that her husband had accepted presidential candidate Dwight D. Eisenhower's offer to be his running mate. "That bite of sandwich popped right out of my mouth," she recalled. She was not eager to become the Second Lady of the Land.

CHAPTER FOUR

The Second Lady of the Land

✦ ✦ ✦ ✦ ✦ ✦ ✦ ✦ ✦ ✦ ✦ ✦ ✦ ✦ ✦ ✦

"You can't think of resigning. If you do, Eisenhower will lose. He can put you off the ticket if he wants to but if you, in the face of attack, do not fight back but simply crawl away, you will destroy yourself," Pat told her husband six weeks before the 1952 election. Newspaper headlines were charging that vice-presidential candidate Nixon had a secret political fund. They claimed that he used it to buy personal luxuries for himself and his family. Fearing a scandal, Republican leaders were pressuring Richard to withdraw from the election. Pat knew the charges were untrue. Some businessmen had simply set up a fund to

✦ ✦ ✦ ✦ ✦ ✦ ✦ ✦ ✦ ✦ ✦ ✦ ✦ ✦ ✦ ✦

Pat sat next to Richard as he gave a televised speech explaining about his controversial political fund.

pay for Richard's trips to his California district, where he gave speeches and met with constituents.

Richard went on television to explain about the fund. Just before the broadcast, he turned nervously to Pat saying, "I just don't think I can go through with this one." Pat replied, "Of course you can." She took his hand, and they walked onto the set. Keeping her feelings to herself, she sat beside her husband, loyally watching him as he spoke. She was unhappy that he had to "parade how little we

Because Nixon mentioned Checkers, the family dog, his televised explanation of the political fund was always referred to as the Checkers Speech.

have and how much we owe in front of all those millions of people." It was necessary, however, if he were to remain in public life. He mentioned Pat, noting with pride that she had worked in his office without pay. He pointed out that she didn't "have a mink coat, but she does have a respectable Republican cloth coat." Then, after saying he did not want to quit, he claimed that his wife was not a quitter either because she was Irish —"and you know the Irish never quit." Because he claimed that Checkers, his daughters' pet dog, was the only gift he ever accepted, reporters called his talk the Checkers Speech.

Nixon received widespread public support after the speech. Yet, Eisenhower hesitated before publicly endorsing his running mate. Pat was furious. "What more does the man want?" she snapped. From that point on, she began to hate politics. Nevertheless, by the time Eisenhower

First Pets

★ ★

As a vice-presidential dog, Checkers joins a long list of executive pets. In the nineteenth century, John Quincy Adams raised silkworms and Andrew Johnson kept white mice. Theodore Roosevelt is famous for loving bear cubs. He had several at the executive mansion, along with a young lion. Dogs have been most popular over the years. Franklin Delano Roosevelt's beloved Scottie, Fala, slept on a special chair in the president's bedroom. At least two presidents had Irish setters: the Trumans called theirs Mike, and the Nixons named theirs King Timahoe. President Harding owned Laddie Boy, an airedale. Lyndon Johnson's beagles, Him and Her, were much photographed. The Ford family's golden retriever, Liberty, gave birth to nine pups in the White House. Of several Bush springer spaniels, Millie was most famous, authoring a book with her owner. Socks, the Clinton's cat, was the first feline to move into the executive mansion in many years.

Tricia (left) and Julie Nixon wore huge campaign buttons in this picture taken with their mother during the 1952 presidential campaign. Republican presidential candidate Dwight Eisenhower was nicknamed "Ike."

and Nixon were swept into office on Election Day, she had put her feelings aside and became a highly effective Second Lady of the Land.

During Richard's first term as vice president, the Nixons moved to a more spacious house in an upper-class section of Washington. Pat now had access to some household help. Nevertheless, she still insisted on planning meals, shopping at the supermarket, and cooking. On foreign trips, she even continued to press her husband's trousers, explaining, "He scolds me, but I've always done it, and I like to." Pat had done these chores for so long that they had become habits she could not easily change.

Pat wanted to create a normal family life for her daughters, but she was fighting a losing battle. Although Richard tried to be home for dinner a few nights a week, he saw Tricia and Julie mostly at breakfast time. Pat and Richard quarreled over the demands of his schedule. She confessed to a friend, "We don't have as many good times as we used to."

Pat was also pressured by the demands of Washington social life and the needs of her children. For example, at a White House luncheon for the wives of the president's Cabinet members (the heads of government departments), Pat asked First Lady Mamie Eisenhower for permission to leave early. She wanted to pick up her children at school. Normally, no one left until the president's wife indicated that the party was over.

As part of her official duties, Pat took charge of the Tuesday meetings of the Senate Ladies Luncheon Club. The members were relatives of present and one-time senators who met to roll bandages for the American Red Cross.

Vice President Richard Nixon bought this home in Washington's fashionable Spring Valley section.

The Nixons enjoyed spending the Christmas holidays in their spacious new home.

53

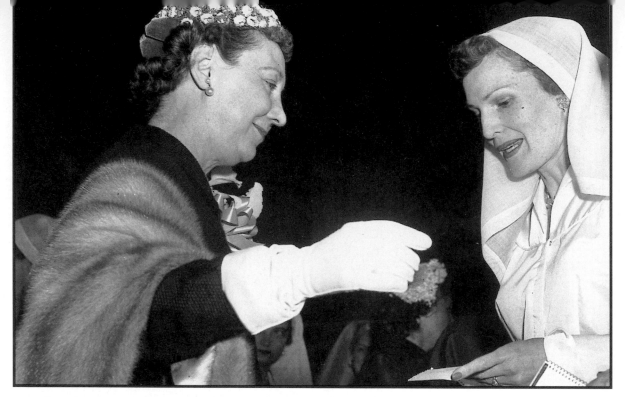

Second Lady Patricia Nixon, dressed in a Red Cross uniform, greets First Lady Mamie Eisenhower, who was guest of honor at the Senate Ladies Luncheon Club.

The vice presidential couple (center) hosted a state dinner in honor of Italian president Giovanni Gronchi (left) and his wife in 1953. At the right is Clare Booth Luce, U.S. ambassador to Italy.

"Help Can't Wait"

★ ★

In 1881, the American Red Cross rose from the ashes of a forest fire. Since 1859, a movement in Europe had been stirring to organize an international body to care for wounded soldiers on the battlefield. Amazingly, no such group existed, and supporters proposed a nonmilitary volunteer organization that would not take sides and would be safe from attack. The United States refused to participate, however, not wanting to become involved in a European venture. Dismayed, nurse Clara Barton organized a Red Cross in the United States in 1881, hoping to change minds. Clara struggled with the cause until a huge forest fire in Michigan left thousands of people homeless and injured. Her fledgling group raised $80,000 in relief money. Red Cross help after a flood along the Ohio River did the final convincing. In 1882, the United States joined Europe in its efforts to establish an International Red Cross. Today, the American Red Cross has approximately 1,650 chapters.

As the Second Lady of the Land, Pat joined her husband for an endless round of diplomatic parties and receptions. She also filled in for the First Lady when needed. Mamie Eisenhower praised her, saying, "I never hesitated to ask her to substitute. She was always gracious and she never put on airs."

On September 24, 1955, the Nixons were called on to substitute for the Eisenhowers under dramatic circumstances. President Eisenhower had suffered a heart attack. The Nixons put in fourteen- to sixteen-hour days. Richard carried on the business of government without appearing to take over the president's job. In addition to their own duties, the vice presidential couple filled in for the Eisenhowers by entertaining foreign officials. At the same time, Pat coped with reporters camped outside her home awaiting news. She invited

55

The Nixons (left) filled in for the Eisenhowers after the president suffered a heart attack in September 1955. Here, they are greeting the president of Guatemala, Carlos Castillo-Armas, and his wife as they arrive for a state visit. In the background is Major General Lionel C. McGarr, U.S. aide to Armas.

them to use the basement playroom as their headquarters and brought them endless pots of hot coffee. It wasn't until the beginning of November, when Eisenhower returned to Washington, that the Nixons could enjoy their privacy once more. This experience prepared them to handle the president's other illnesses.

With the approach of the 1956 presidential elections, Republican leaders urged Eisenhower to replace his running mate. Much as Pat hated the prospect of another campaign, she

Richard Nixon's father, Frank, died in September 1956, during the Eisenhower–Nixon campaign for a second term in office. After the funeral (left to right), the vice president's mother Hannah, brother Edward, Richard, and brother Don leave the East Whittier Friends Church.

encouraged her husband to fight for his renomination. She told a family friend, "No one is going to push us off the ticket." When Richard succeeded, he and Pat were not able to celebrate his victory. They were at the bedside of Richard's father, who was seriously ill. Frank Nixon died on September 4, 1956. Two weeks later, the Nixons were on the campaign trail, often visiting two states in one day. When asked how they did it, Pat smiled grimly and said, "We killed ourselves."

The Nixon's travels were not limited to election times. During his two terms in office, President Eisenhower

Vice President Richard Nixon (left) and Second Lady Patricia speak to a Cambodian girl at the Angor Wat ruins during the Nixons' tour of Asia.

asked them to make many goodwill trips abroad. They went to Asia, Africa, Europe, and South America. As a young woman, Pat had always dreamed of visiting foreign lands. As an adult, she became the most well-traveled Second Lady in the nation's history. She was also well informed. In preparation for each trip, she read about the countries she'd see. At each place she stayed, she astonished the household staffs by doing her own personal laundry and fixing her own hair, now blonde. She surprised her hosts by asking to be taken to hospitals, orphanages, and schools instead of for-

In 1957, the Nixons bought this elegant home in the Wesley Heights section of Washington.

mal luncheons and receptions. Pat was not a member of any feminist groups that demanded equal social and political rights for women. Yet, she deliberately met with women's groups in every country she visited. She wanted to spotlight their achievements and point out their problems. "Everywhere I went, it helped women."

One goodwill trip, a visit to several South American countries, turned into a nightmare. On May 13, 1958, in

Pat visits a child at a Warsaw hospital during the Nixons' visit to the Soviet Union and Poland in 1959.

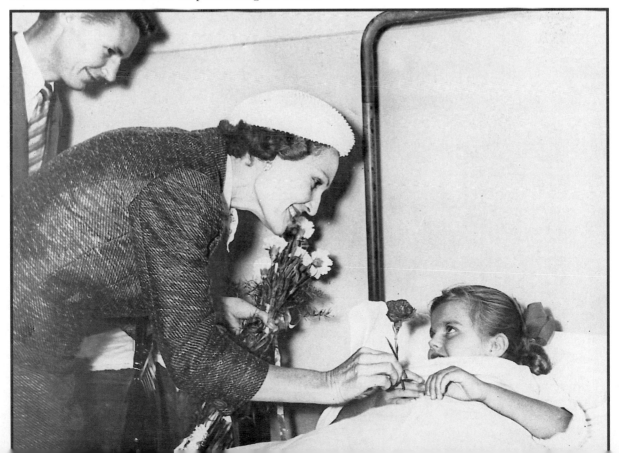

During a 1958 good-will trip to South America, angry mobs attacked the Nixon motorcade in Caracas, Venezuela.

Caracas, Venezuela, the Nixon motorcade was unexpectedly attacked by angry mobs. The Nixons were traveling from the airport in two separate limousines. The police disappeared when a group of demonstrators blocked the vice president's car and attacked it. Other demonstrators surrounded Pat's car, throwing rocks and pounding on the roof with clubs. She tried to calm her companion, the foreign minister's wife. "We got a few good knocks on our car, but that didn't frighten me," Pat said. Finally, the Nixon cars broke free of the crowds and headed for safety at the United States Embassy. The planned ceremonies were abandoned. The vice presidential couple returned to Washington to be welcomed as heroes by the president and other officials. Commenting later on the incident, the vice president noted that his wife was "probably the coolest person in the whole party." As she always did, Pat kept her emotions in check.

The Nixons watch on television as Oregon's governor, Mark Hatfield, announces that Richard will be the Republican candidate for president in the 1960 election.

During the next eight years, Pat's self-control was sorely tested. In 1960, Richard asked her to sacrifice her privacy once again to support his bid for the presidency. Although she bitterly objected to his decision, she campaigned enthusiastically for him.

Some critics complained that Pat was too involved in her husband's campaign. She told reporters that she was like "women all over America taking an active part, not only in political life, but in all activities." On election night, photos revealed the tears in her

Television Wins an Election

✫ ✫ ✫ ✫ ✫ ✫ ✫ ✫ ✫ ✫ ✫ ✫ ✫ ✫ ✫ ✫ ✫ ✫ ✫ ✫

Television took the country by storm in the 1950s. By the end of the decade, watching TV had become America's favorite pastime. Many families spent hours a day in front of the "boob tube." No wonder television played its first major role in a presidential election in 1960. That year, Richard Nixon faced the relatively unknown Democrat John F. Kennedy in the race for the White House. When Kennedy suggested a series of televised debates, front-runner Nixon agreed. Under the bright lights of the first debate, however, Nixon—who had refused makeup—appeared pale, nervous, and uncomfortable. He had just been released from the hospital after treatment for an infected knee. John Kennedy looked sun-tanned and relaxed. The contrast between the two men stunned many of the 77 million viewers. They voted for the confident young Kennedy, who won the election. Interestingly, Nixon impressed those who had heard the debate only on the radio.

With Pat on the verge of tears, Richard Nixon gives a concession speech, acknowledging that it looked as if Democrat John F. Kennedy had won the 1960 presidential election.

In September 1967, the Nixon family returned briefly to California from their home in New York City to attend the funeral of Richard's mother, Hannah. Shown here are Pat, Richard, and their daughter Julie.

eyes when Richard lost the race to Democrat John F. Kennedy by only a little more than 100,000 votes. Pat wanted her husband to demand a recount, but he refused.

The Nixons moved to Los Angeles where Richard joined a law firm. For the first time in fifteen years, Pat had unlimited time to devote to her daughters and her own interests. She enjoyed gardening, swimming, and shopping. Then, in the fall of 1961, Richard asked his family whether he should run for governor of California

in 1962. Pat was firmly against it, but she eventually gave in, saying "I am once more a candidate's wife—and proud to be, too." When Richard was defeated by Edmund "Pat" Brown, he publicly vowed never to run again.

Pat told friends she was glad to leave politics, to be "out of the rat race." Richard became a partner in a New York law firm, and the family moved East in 1963. During their stay in New York, Pat enjoyed life as a private citizen. She had time to prepare meals for her family, to visit depart-

Here, Pat is shown in the Nixons' New York apartment on Fifth Avenue.

ment stores, or even drop in at her husband's office to help out. In September 1967, the Nixons returned briefly to California for the funeral of Hannah Nixon.

In 1968, Pat heartily approved of Richard's decision to run for president again. She wanted him to overcome his 1960 defeat. In interviews, she praised him as a family man but refused to talk about campaign issues. She explained, "The candidate should speak for himself." Pat always

The Nixons at a rally with New York governor Nelson Rockefeller during the 1968 presidential campaign

appeared calm in public, listening attentively to Richard's speeches with a fixed smile on her face. This is why her critics called her "Plastic Pat." Yet, in personal conversations she was lively, gracious, and warm.

On election night, there were tears of joy in her eyes when Richard defeated Democrat Hubert H. Humphrey. Throughout her marriage, Pat always sacrificed her dreams of privacy to her husband's political ambitions. Now, Richard had finally realized his dream. As a result, Pat was going to live in the White House as the First Lady of the Land.

☆ ☆ ☆ ☆ ☆ ☆ ☆ ☆ ☆ ☆ ☆ ☆ ☆ ☆ ☆ ☆

First Lady

✫ ✫ ✫ ✫ ✫ ✫ ✫ ✫ ✫ ✫ ✫ ✫ ✫ ✫

"People are my project," Pat announced to one reporter. As First Lady, she was determined to help people at home and abroad. She spent four to five hours a day going through the mail, reading many of the fifteen hundred letters that arrived each month. She answered more letters than any other First Lady. She refused to use an "autopen" and personally signed all the mail sent from her office. She knew what mail from the White House could mean to ordinary citizens. "It's shown to all the neighbors, and often published in the local paper. It's important to people who receive it." If the letter writer seemed desperate, Pat or her staff offered assistance.

✫ ✫ ✫ ✫ ✫ ✫ ✫ ✫ ✫ ✫ ✫ ✫ ✫ ✫

On this page: The busy life of a First Lady in her role as the nation's hostess

Left: Pat Nixon hosts a tea at the White House
Below: The Nixons entertain the Duke and Duchess of Windsor at a formal White House dinner.

Below: Patricia Nixon (right) escorts Mrs. Harold Wilson, wife of the British prime minister, to a state dinner honoring the Wilsons.

First Lady Patricia Nixon checks with the White House chefs as they prepare a 1969 Thanksgiving Day dinner for 225 senior citizens.

In the 1940s and 1950s, most First Ladies devoted themselves to their duties as the nation's hostess. Following their example, during her first three years, Pat entertained a record-breaking 109,000 guests at formal dinners, teas, luncheons, and receptions. She included average citizens in official functions. In 1969, she invited 225 elderly residents of Washington nursing homes and homes for the aged to Thanksgiving dinner at the White House. She also arranged for nondenominational religious services to be held on Sundays in the East Room. These were attended

Pat Nixon is shown here as she greets women journalists and writers at the White House in 1971.

by working people as well as government officials. Pat was the first First Lady to hold a press conference since the 1940s. She even invited the female reporters assigned to her to a luncheon in the State Dining Room. She respected the working press and

made herself available to them. Her comments, however, were not very revealing. Of course, for Pat, the most memorable social event during her years as First Lady was the June 1971 wedding of her daughter Tricia to Edward F. Cox in the Rose Garden of the White House.

Pat wanted to make the White House more welcoming and interesting to tourists. She felt that it belonged to all the people. At her suggestion, the White House was lit outside at night. She had the White House security guards trained to be helpful and courteous to sightseers. She began tours of the White House gardens. Pamphlets were written to describe the rooms. These were translated into other languages to assist foreign visitors. For tourists waiting in line to see the mansion, Pat installed large display cases and included historic items usually kept in the family quarters. Because of her concern for the needs of the disabled, ramps were installed for the wheelchair bound, and the blind were given permission to touch what others saw. Since working people could not come during the

A Wedding to Remember

✮ ✮

Tricia Nixon's wedding to Edward Cox in the White House Rose Garden was truly a national affair. The U.S. Army Strings, the U.S. Marine Corps Harp and Flute Duo, and the U.S. Air Force String Ensemble provided the music. The American Association of Nurserymen donated hundreds of flowering plants and trees from six states, including 1,500 cut white roses. Before the big day, chefs of the *New York Times* and the *Washington Post* tested the recipe for the 350-pound (159-kilogram) lemon wedding cake, decorated with lovebirds and standing 7 feet (2 meters) tall. The Reverend Billy Graham could not prevent the rain that fell on the first-ever Rose Garden wedding, although he said he'd been using "all the power he had to make it stop." President and father-of-the-bride Richard Nixon hoped that the rain might make people remember the day more. Indeed, one guest remarked it had felt as if she'd been "sitting on a wet sponge."

Newlyweds Tricia Nixon and Edward Cox on their wedding day in the White House Rose Garden

Art historian Clement Conger (*above*) helped Pat
redecorate the White House.

day, she opened the mansion to the public at night during the Christmas season. For the first time in about fifty years, the First Lady personally greeted lines of visitors, shaking their hands and posing for pictures with them. In 1970, the number of White House tourists broke all records.

Under the direction of art historian Clement Conger, Pat redecorated the White House. When she became First Lady, only one-third of the furnishings were genuine antiques. The rest were copies. By the time she left,

Pat Nixon shows off the newly refurbished White House Blue Room to reporters in May 1972.

Pat poses in the newly redecorated White House Red Room.

The Green Room was also refurbished during Pat Nixon's term as First Lady.

The evening before her fifty-seventh birthday, Pat Nixon entertained wives of newspapermen and officials who were at the Gridiron dinner.

two-thirds of the furnishings were real antiques. Through private funds, gifts, and loans, valuable furniture and works of art were brought to the mansion. Pat avoided publicizing her achievements, preferring to let Jackie Kennedy have the credit for restoring the White House as a historic mansion. In 1971, she even invited Jackie and her children for a private viewing of newly installed portraits of President and Mrs. Kennedy. Jackie was delighted with the changes Pat was planning and wrote her that the visit was "a moving experience."

In the 1960s, First Ladies were not just gracious hostesses. They were expected to involve themselves in issues and causes. Instead of limiting herself to one area, Pat chose to sponsor "volunteerism" to express her concern for people. "This is where I think I can help," she declared, "encouraging what my husband has called those 'small splendid efforts' of people trying to make life better for others." In 1969, Pat traveled around the nation drawing attention to community projects such as day-care centers for migrant workers' children and ghetto gardens. At the White House, she welcomed local groups and gave recognition to outstanding individual volunteers.

In 1970, Pat made a second volunteerism tour, traveling 4,130 miles (6,646 km) and visiting many colleges and universities. One undergraduate who heard her speak about volunteerism told reporters, "I felt this is a woman who really cares about what we are doing." She wanted to show that not all college students were protesters. Whenever Pat appeared in public, she was taunted by youthful demonstrators. They wanted the United States to withdraw immediately from the Vietnam War. Since the mid-1960s, American troops had been

On one of her volunteerism tours, Pat Nixon painted a picture with a child at the Forest Grove Day Nursery in Portland, Oregon.

Pat helped turn the jump rope at the Follow-Through Center in Lafayette, Colorado, one of the stops on her tour of college volunteer work in the state.

trying to prevent Communist North Vietnam from taking control of South Vietnam. President Nixon was attempting to negotiate an end to the war.

As a result of the war, Pat became the second presidential wife to tour a combat zone. In 1969, she accompanied her husband to Vietnam. Avoiding formal social events, she insisted on being flown in a helicopter over 18 miles (29 km) of enemy-

Vietnam War: Fast Facts

WHAT: Conflict over control of the Southeast Asian nation of Vietnam

WHEN: 1957–1975

WHO: The United States, South Vietnam, and various allies opposed the North Vietnamese and the Viet Cong.

WHERE: Throughout North and South Vietnam, and later into Cambodia and Laos

WHY: In the early 1950s, the French controlled Vietnam. Fearing a Communist takeover of Vietnam and the rest of Southeast Asia, American leaders supported the French. When the French withdrew, the United States sent military advisers to help train the South Vietnamese to oppose the Communist north. America became more and more involved until U.S. troops were actually fighting alongside the South Vietnamese in a war against North Vietnam.

OUTCOME: Direct American military involvement ended with a cease-fire in 1973. In all, 58,000 American soldiers and about 1 million North and South Vietnamese perished. In 1975, the North invaded the South, and the capital of Saigon surrendered. Today, a unified Vietnam lives under Communist rule.

In July 1969, Pat Nixon flew over miles of enemy-held territory before her helicopter arrived at a military hospital near Saigon.

infested jungle to a military hospital. Instead of attending a doctor's lecture on how the place was run, she insisted, "I want to see the boys." She went from bed to bed talking with the wounded and promising to write letters to their parents.

Moved by what she saw, Pat refused to let war protests interfere with her activities as First Lady. During a May 1971 demonstration, she said, "We are not going to buckle to these people." Because of the widespread protests, however, the graduations of daughter Julie and son-in-law David Eisenhower had to be celebrated privately. (Not wishing a White House wedding, they had decided to

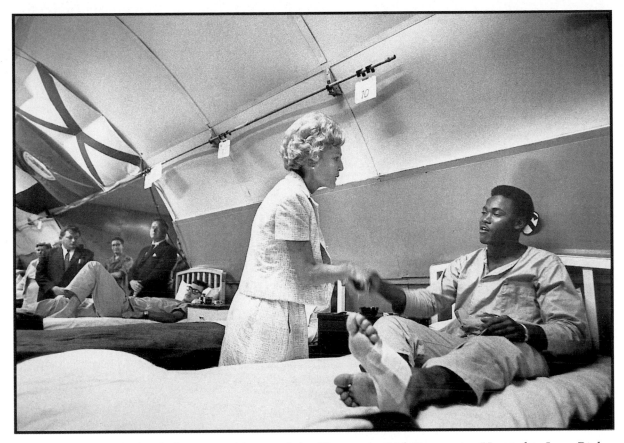

Patricia went from bed to bed visiting with wounded soldiers at the 24th Evacuation Hospital in Long Binh, South Vietnam.

be married December 22, 1968, in New York.)

Pat held feminist views on a number of women's issues that were being widely discussed in the 1970s, but she urged feminists to appeal to Congress for change instead of protesting conditions. Looking back on her personal experience in the working world, Pat thought "It was time to formally recognize that women in employment and other areas deserved equal treatment with men." This is why she supported the movement to have the Equal Rights Amendment added to the Constitution, a position also taken by some other Republicans. Pat approved the change that let women

Pat Nixon visited the national orphanage near Saigon during her tour of South Vietnam. Here, she shakes hands with a young Vietnamese orphan.

Partly because of her interest in women's issues throughout the world, Pat hosted a group of foreign students from Smith College who visited the White House in 1970.

serve as military social aides at White House functions, a tour of duty previously restricted to men. She also endorsed the Women's Political Caucus's goal of getting more women elected to office "even if they were not Republicans." In 1971, Pat was the first First Lady to publicly ask her husband to appoint a woman to the Supreme Court. "Our population is more than 50 percent women, so why not?" She was disappointed when her wish was denied.

To Richard, Pat was a wife, not a

The Equal Rights Amendment

☆ ☆

The Equal Rights Amendment that Pat Nixon supported in 1972 was never added to the Constitution. First written in 1923, it stated that men and women shall have the same rights under the law. The amendment was approved by Congress in 1972. To become law, it would also need to be ratified (approved) by 38 states by the 1982 deadline. Only 35 states approved the amendment before the deadline. Why would people vote against such a basic statement of equal treatment for men and women? Some feared that the amendment would force a negative change in the traditional roles of women. Many people believed that it would threaten family life and marriage. The industries that saved money by employing cheaper female labor lobbied against the ERA. Some women believed they would lose protections already in the law if the ERA passed. Others were concerned about women being drafted into military service. A few even predicted that men and women would have to share public bathrooms. One very vocal critic, Phyllis Schlafly, organized an emotional campaign against the ERA. She reinforced all of these fears and took advantage of the fact that few Americans understood how the ERA would change their daily lives. In fact, women in states that adopted similar amendments to their state constitutions won victories in areas of equal pay, more varied work and educational opportunities, and property ownership.

At the annual White House Christmas party, Pat is surrounded by children of foreign diplomats stationed in Washington.

political adviser. She read the newspapers and briefing reports regularly and had her own views of politics and politicians. He, however, rarely consulted her. In the White House, he separated his political life from his family life. Nevertheless, he phoned Pat during the day to praise her work, surprised her with gifts, and enjoyed the private family dinners she scheduled. She bowed to his request that she not be photographed in a bathing suit, even though other First Ladies had. Yet, when pants suits became fashionable, she wore them in public although he disliked them.

Richard usually did not interfere when his staff, housed in the West Wing of the White House, tried to control Pat's staff in the East Wing. His staff also attempted to limit the First Lady's appearances with her husband. Often, they waited until the last minute to tell her about the president's trips and failed to include her. Then, if she wanted to go, she would have to appeal directly to her husband. When she brought such incidents to her husband's attention, he usually supported her. More frequently, however, Pat chose to fight her own battles. For example, presidential assistants might order ugly bleacher seats for the Sunday morning prayer services, but she did not have to use them. Pat might let her husband's aides remove her press secretaries, but she insisted that the replacements be women.

Pat's interest in people reached beyond the borders of the United States. She was the most widely traveled First Lady, visiting 83 countries and covering 108,000 miles (173,804 km). In May 1970, when an earthquake devastated Peru, Pat set out on a personal mission of mercy. She traveled to Peru, bringing much-needed supplies and medical help. She personally toured stricken areas with the Peruvian president's wife. She hugged homeless townspeople as she walked past mountains of rubble and twisted beams. The Peruvian press praised her. "In her human warmth and identification with the suffering of the Peruvian people, she has gone beyond the norms of international courtesy . . ." Relations between the governments of Peru and the United States were much improved after her visit.

Pat Nixon hugged a young girl upon her arrival in Peru on a mission of mercy after the devastating earthquake of May 1970.

Pat walks through the ruins of a cathedral in Huaraz, Peru, that was destroyed by the 1970 earthquake. Joining her on this tour of the destruction is Mrs. Juan Velasco Alvarado, wife of the president of Peru.

Ghanian drummers welcome Pat Nixon to Accra during her tour of West Africa in 1972.

Pat shakes hands with painted children at an orphanage in Bingerville, Ivory Coast.

In 1972, Pat became the only First Lady to travel to Africa. As her husband's representative, she attended swearing-in ceremonies for the president of Liberia. She also met with the leaders of Ghana and the Ivory Coast, nations she also visited. She had mixed very naturally with both black people and white people in Africa. Africans were delighted that she willingly tried on a native dress and joined in a tribal dance. Her visit was an enormous success for the Nixon administration.

In 1972, Pat became the first First Lady to visit Communist China. She so charmed the Chinese leader Chou En-lai that he presented her with two pandas for the National Zoo. In the Soviet Union (now the Commonwealth of Independent States and Russia), she followed the same practices she started as Second Lady. Instead of formalities, she met the

Pat Nixon being escorted through the Imperial City in Peking (now spelled Beijing) during the Nixons' 1972 trip to China

people in factories, on farms, in subways, and at schools. She toured with the leaders' wives, giving them press coverage they usually were denied.

Pat was sent out on the campaign trail by herself when her husband ran for reelection in 1972. She toured seven midwestern and western states, saying, "I'm taking the White House to the people." She endured fierce heat in Riverside, California, gale-force winds in Billings, Montana, and a sleet storm in Yellowstone National Park. "I do or die. I never cancel out," she said.

Pat paid little attention to a newspaper story in June 1972 about a bungled burglary at Democratic National Headquarters in the Watergate

Patricia Nixon, touring with the wives of Soviet leaders, met the people on a Moscow subway during her trip to the Soviet Union in 1972.

An Exotic Gift

★ ★

The scientific name for giant pandas, *Ailuropoda melanoleuca,* means "black and white cat-footed animal." Their feet are indeed interesting because their enlarged wristbones act as a thumb, helping them grasp the bamboo stalks that they love to eat. By far the most famous pandas are Ling-Ling and Hsing-Hsing, presented to the Nixons by the People's Republic of China in 1972. The two lived together at the  National Zoological Park in Washington, D.C., until Ling-Ling died in 1992. She was the oldest panda to live in a zoo up to that time. Her mate continues to eat many pounds of bamboo each day, along with fresh produce and rice.

Complex. Members of Nixon's reelection campaign had secretly masterminded the break-in. Reporters began to question her about the growing scandal. She replied, "I only know what I read in the newspapers." Alarmed, Pat asked Richard whether the stories were true. He denied them. For the rest of the campaign, Pat insisted that the burglary "has been blown out of proportion." Although her husband won a second term of office, the Watergate scandal soon made Pat a private citizen once again.

★ ★ ★ ★ ★ ★ ★ ★ ★ ★ ★ ★ ★ ★ ★ ★

CHAPTER SIX

A Private Citizen

☆ ☆ ☆ ☆ ☆ ☆ ☆ ☆ ☆ ☆ ☆ ☆ ☆ ☆ ☆ ☆ ☆

"I would have burned or destroyed [the tapes] because they were like a private diary, not public property," Pat told a longtime friend. In July 1973, along with the American public, Pat was amazed to learn that her husband had taped his private conversations about the Watergate break-in and other matters. Government prosecutors and members of Congress demanded the tapes. Pat did not think Richard should supply evidence against himself. He recognized, however, that he would be removed from office if he did not give them up.

When edited versions of the tapes were released in

☆ ☆ ☆ ☆ ☆ ☆ ☆ ☆ ☆ ☆ ☆ ☆ ☆ ☆ ☆ ☆ ☆

Richard Nixon bid a televised farewell to his Whitte House staff after he resigned from the presidency.

Newspaper headlines all over the country announced Nixon's resignation. This is the front page of the Friday, August 9, 1974, edition of the New York Times.

April 1974, Pat spent twelve hours reading all 1,254 pages. She learned little about Watergate, but Richard's swearing and crude language shocked her. This was not the man she knew. Yet she joked in private about how the swearwords would have sounded in the Boston accent of President John Kennedy or the southwestern twang of President Lyndon Johnson. In May, when asked whether Richard would resign, Pat replied, "Why should he? There's no reason to." She still did not know that Richard had been lying to conceal his aides' involvement in the Watergate break-in. She believed that it was "all politics and will go away."

In July, to comply with a Supreme Court decision, Richard released additional tapes. These showed how he plotted with his advisers to stop the FBI's investigation of Watergate. When she read copies of these tapes, a saddened and hurt Pat withdrew into herself. She even refused to take phone calls from longtime friends. When the House Judiciary Committee voted to remove Nixon from office, he decided to resign. He did not consult his wife in advance. He knew

she would want him to fight on, if only to narrow the charges against himself. By then, he had isolated himself from his family and all but his closest advisors.

Once she was informed of his decision, Pat began packing up the family's belongings. Two days later, as the family walked toward the East Room for Richard to bid farewell to his staff, she gasped, "Oh, Dick, you can't have it televised." He explained, "We owe it to our supporters." Pat's pain was etched on her face as she listened to her husband's speech. He paid tribute to his mother, but not once did he mention Pat. He claimed that if he had, he would not have been able to continue. Later, he wrote, "She had given so much to the nation and so much to the world. Now she would have to share my exile. She deserved so much more."

Escorted by Gerald Ford and his wife Betty, the Nixons walked to a waiting helicopter that would take them from the White House to Andrews Air Force Base. From there, they flew to California in the presidential plane. The Nixons kept to

The Nixons (on the right) were escorted by the Fords (on the left) as they walked to the helicopter that would take Pat and Richard away from the White House.

Gerald R. Ford (1913–   )

✫ ✫

Gerald Ford was the first American to become both the vice president and the president without being elected. Here's why. Vice President Spiro T. Agnew resigned his position in October of 1973 when charged with not paying certain taxes. President Nixon chose the likable Gerald Ford, then serving as House minority leader, to take his place. Born in 1913, young Ford had made his name as a football star at the University of Michigan. Then, twenty-five years as a congressman earned him a reputation among both Democrats and Republicans as trustworthy and honest. Nixon's resignation in the wake of the Watergate scandal thrust Ford into the presidency. He began his brief two years in office by pardoning Richard Nixon. Over the following months, Ford proved to be very conservative and not terribly effective as president. Democratic peanut farmer Jimmy Carter defeated him in the 1976 election.

An aerial view of the Nixons' San Clemente residence, Casa Pacifica

themselves in San Clemente. They lived in Casa Pacifica, a home they had purchased in 1969. Pat spent her days gardening and reading while Richard grew more and more depressed. Even when President Ford pardoned him for any crimes he might have committed, Richard's mood did not lighten. Pat comforted him. Later in the month, he entered the hospital with a serious blood disorder. While he recuperated from surgery in October, Pat was at his bedside. Each day, she encouraged him, telling him to look forward to new achievements and to take pride in all he had done for his country.

Richard recovered his health, but Pat's began to fail. On July 7, 1976, she suffered a stroke, a blood clot in the brain. Her left side was paralyzed, but her speech was unaffected. Slowly, she learned to walk again. A quarter of a million pieces of mail were sent to the hospital wishing her well. Pat made sure that the many flowers she received were given to hospital patients. When she was discharged, Richard pushed her wheelchair to the waiting car. To the press, Pat said, "I

Daughters Tricia (left) and Julie accompanied their parents when Pat left the hospital after having suffered a stroke in 1976.

In 1982, Pat and Richard attended a performance of the Ringling Brothers circus with their daughter Julie and her children.

feel fine," and then joked, referring to Richard, "but I'm a little frightened about the driver." Pat worked very hard to regain the use of her left arm.

The Nixons wanted to spend more time with their four young grandchildren: Christopher Cox, and Melanie, Jennifer, and Alex Eisenhower. In 1980, Pat and Richard moved back to the East Coast, first to New York and then to New Jersey. Richard was now treated as an elder statesman, consult-

ed on world affairs by the nation's leaders. Pat's public appearances were rare, but she did advise Nancy Reagan by phone about the First Lady's planned trip to China. Pat's health continued to decline. In August 1983, she had a minor stroke. The following summer, she developed a lung infection. From then on, she was in and out of hospitals. On June 22, 1993, the day after the Nixons celebrated their fifty-third wedding anniversary, Pat died of lung cancer. She was buried on the grounds of the Nixon Library in Yorba Linda, California. Richard died of a stroke on April 22, 1994, and was laid to rest beside her. Pat's achievements as First Lady were impressive, but her devotion and loyalty to her husband were even more admirable.

Richard and Patricia Nixon are buried side by side at the Richard Nixon Library and Birthplace in Yorba Linda, California.

Presidents and Their First Ladies

| YEARS IN OFFICE | | | | |
President	Birth–Death	First Lady		Birth–Death
1789–1797				
George Washington	1732–1799	Martha Dandridge Custis Washington		1731–1802
1797–1801				
John Adams	1735–1826	Abigail Smith Adams		1744–1818
1801–1809				
Thomas Jefferson†	1743–1826			
1809–1817				
James Madison	1751–1836	Dolley Payne Todd Madison		1768–1849
1817–1825				
James Monroe	1758–1831	Elizabeth Kortright Monroe		1768–1830
1825–1829				
John Quincy Adams	1767–1848	Louisa Catherine Johnson Adams		1775–1852
1829–1837				
Andrew Jackson†	1767–1845	Rachel Donelson Jackson		1767–1828
1837–1841				
Martin Van Buren†	1782–1862			
1841				
William Henry Harrison‡	1773–1841			
1841–1845				
John Tyler	1790–1862	Letitia Christian Tyler (1841–1842)		1790–1842
		Julia Gardiner Tyler (1844–1845)		1820–1889
1845–1849				
James K. Polk	1795–1849	Sarah Childress Polk		1803–1891
1849–1850				
Zachary Taylor	1784–1850	Margaret Mackall Smith Taylor		1788–1852
1850–1853				
Millard Fillmore	1800–1874	Abigail Powers Fillmore		1798–1853
1853–1857				
Franklin Pierce	1804–1869	Jane Means Appleton Pierce		1806–1863
1857–1861				
James Buchanan*	1791–1868			
1861–1865				
Abraham Lincoln	1809–1865	Mary Todd Lincoln		1818–1882
1865–1869				
Andrew Johnson	1808–1875	Eliza McCardle Johnson		1810–1876
1869–1877				
Ulysses S. Grant	1822–1885	Julia Dent Grant		1826–1902
1877–1881				
Rutherford B. Hayes	1822–1893	Lucy Ware Webb Hayes		1831–1889
1881				
James A. Garfield	1831–1881	Lucretia Rudolph Garfield		1832–1918
1881–1885				
Chester A. Arthur†	1829–1886			

† wife died before he took office   ‡ wife too ill to accompany him to Washington   * never married

1885–1889			
Grover Cleveland	1837–1908	Frances Folsom Cleveland	1864–1947
1889–1893			
Benjamin Harrison	1833–1901	Caroline Lavinia Scott Harrison	1832–1892
1893–1897			
Grover Cleveland	1837–1908	Frances Folsom Cleveland	1864–1947
1897–1901			
William McKinley	1843–1901	Ida Saxton McKinley	1847–1907
1901–1909			
Theodore Roosevelt	1858–1919	Edith Kermit Carow Roosevelt	1861–1948
1909–1913			
William Howard Taft	1857–1930	Helen Herron Taft	1861–1943
1913–1921			
Woodrow Wilson	1856–1924	Ellen Louise Axson Wilson (1913–1914)	1860–1914
		Edith Bolling Galt Wilson (1915–1921)	1872–1961
1921–1923			
Warren G. Harding	1865–1923	Florence Kling Harding	1860–1924
1923–1929			
Calvin Coolidge	1872–1933	Grace Anna Goodhue Coolidge	1879–1957
1929–1933			
Herbert Hoover	1874–1964	Lou Henry Hoover	1874–1944
1933–1945			
Franklin D. Roosevelt	1882–1945	Anna Eleanor Roosevelt	1884–1962
1945–1953			
Harry S. Truman	1884–1972	Bess Wallace Truman	1885–1982
1953–1961			
Dwight D. Eisenhower	1890–1969	Mamie Geneva Doud Eisenhower	1896–1979
1961–1963			
John F. Kennedy	1917–1963	Jacqueline Bouvier Kennedy	1929–1994
1963–1969			
Lyndon B. Johnson	1908–1973	Claudia Taylor (Lady Bird) Johnson	1912–
1969–1974			
Richard Nixon	1913–1994	Patricia Ryan Nixon	1912–1993
1974–1977			
Gerald Ford	1913–	Elizabeth Bloomer Ford	1918–
1977–1981			
James Carter	1924–	Rosalynn Smith Carter	1927–
1981–1989			
Ronald Reagan	1911–	Nancy Davis Reagan	1923–
1989–1993			
George Bush	1924–	Barbara Pierce Bush	1925–
1993–			
William Jefferson Clinton	1946–	Hillary Rodham Clinton	1947–

Patricia Ryan Nixon
Timeline

1912	★	Thelma Catherine "Pat" Ryan is born on March 16
		Woodrow Wilson is elected president
1913	★	Sixteenth Amendment is added to the Constitution
		Seventeenth Amendment is added to the Constitution
		Richard Milhous Nixon is born
1914	★	World War I begins
1916	★	Woodrow Wilson is reelected president
1917	★	United States enters World War I
1918	★	United States and its allies win World War I
1919	★	Eighteenth Amendment is added to the Constitution
1920	★	U.S. population is 105,710,620
		Warren G. Harding is elected president
		Woodrow Wilson wins the Nobel Peace Prize
		Nineteenth Amendment, which gave women the right to vote, is added to the Constitution
1923	★	Calvin Coolidge becomes president upon the death of Warren G. Harding
1927	★	Charles Lindbergh makes the first nonstop, solo flight across the Atlantic Ocean
1928	★	Herbert Hoover is elected president
1929	★	Stock market crashes and the Great Depression begins
1930	★	U.S. population is 122,775,046
1931	★	"The Star-Spangled Banner" becomes the national anthem
1932	★	Franklin D. Roosevelt is elected president
		Amelia Earhart becomes the first woman to fly solo across the Atlantic Ocean

1933	★	Twentieth Amendment is added to the Constitution
		President Roosevelt begins the New Deal to end the Great Depression
		Twenty-first Amendment is added to the Constitution
1934	★	Nylon is invented
1935	★	Congress passes the Social Security Act
1936	★	Franklin D. Roosevelt is reelected president
1937	★	Patricia Ryan graduates from the University of Southern California
1939	★	World War II begins
1940	★	U.S. population is 131,669,275
		Patricia Ryan marries Richard Milhous Nixon
		Franklin D. Roosevelt is reelected president
1941	★	Japan bombs Pearl Harbor and the United States enters World War II
1942	★	Richard Nixon enlists in the navy
1944	★	Franklin D. Roosevelt is reelected president
1945	★	Franklin D. Roosevelt dies
		Harry S. Truman becomes president
		Germany and Japan surrender, ending World War II
1946	★	Patricia (Tricia) Nixon is born
		Richard M. Nixon is elected to the U.S. House of Representatives
1947	★	Jackie Robinson becomes the first African American to play major-league baseball
1948	★	Julie Nixon is born
		Harry S. Truman is reelected president
1949	★	United Nations headquarters is dedicated in New York City
1950	★	U.S. population is 150,697,361
		United States enters Korean War
		Richard Nixon is elected to the U.S. Senate

1951	★	Twenty-second Amendment is added to the Constitution
1952	★	Dwight D. Eisenhower is elected president
		Richard Nixon is elected vice president
1953	★	Korean War ends
1954	★	Supreme Court declares segregated schools to be unconstitutional
1956	★	Dwight D. Eisenhower is reelected president
		Richard Nixon is reelected vice president
1960	★	U.S. population is 179,245,000
		John F. Kennedy is elected president, defeating Nixon
1961	★	Berlin Wall separates East and West Berlin
		First Americans fly in space
		United States sends aid and troops to South Vietnam
		Twenty-third Amendmenet is added to the Constitution
1962	★	Twenty-fourth Amendment is added to the Constitution
1963	★	John F. Kennedy is assassinated
		Lyndon B. Johnson becomes president
1964	★	Lyndon B. Johnson is elected president
1965	★	Malcolm X is assassinated
		Riots break out in Los Angeles' Watts neighborhood
1966	★	Congress passes the Medicare Act
1967	★	Twenty-fifth Amendment is added to the Constitution
1968	★	Martin Luther King, Jr., and Robert F. Kennedy are assassinated
		Richard M. Nixon is elected president
1969	★	President Nixon withdraws 110,000 soldiers from Vietnam
1970	★	U.S. population is 205,000,000
		Antiwar protests rock college campuses

1971	★	Twenty-sixth Amendment is added to the Constitution
		Tricia Nixon marries Edward Cox at the White House
1972	★	Last U.S. ground troops are withdrawn from Vietnam
		Burglary at the Watergate Complex is reported
		Richard Nixon is reelected president
1973	★	Vice President Spiro Agnew resigns
		Gerald Ford becomes vice president
1974	★	Richard M. Nixon resigns from office
		Gerald Ford becomes president
1975	★	South Vietnam falls to the Communists
1976	★	Jimmy Carter is elected president
1979	★	Iranians seize U.S. Embassy in Tehran and hold American hostages
1980	★	U.S. population is 226,504,825
		Ronald Reagan is elected president
1981	★	Iranians release the U.S. hostages
		Sandra Day O'Connor becomes the first woman appointed to the Supreme Court
1983	★	Sally Ride becomes the first American woman astronaut in space
1984	★	Ronald Reagan is reelected president
1986	★	Space shuttle *Challenger* explodes, killing all on board
1988	★	George Bush is elected president
1989	★	Berlin Wall comes down
1990	★	U.S. population is 263,080,000
1991	★	United States leads allies in Persian Gulf War
		Iraq is pushed from Kuwait
1992	★	Bill Clinton is elected president
		Twenty-seventh Amendment is added to the Constitution
1993	★	Patricia Ryan Nixon dies on June 22

Fast Facts about
Patricia Ryan Nixon

Born: March 16, 1912, in Ely, Nevada

Died: June 22, 1993, at home in Park Ridge, New Jersey

Burial Site: Yorba Linda, California, on the grounds of the Richard M. Nixon Library and Birthplace

Parents: William Ryan and Kate Halberstadt Bender Ryan

Education: Excelsior High School, Fullerton Junior College, and honors degree from the University of Southern California (1937)

Jobs and careers: Janitor and bookkeeper in a bank, secretary, X-ray technician, movie extra, dental assistant, telephone operator, model, high-school business teacher, U.S. government worker

Marriage: To Richard Milhous Nixon on June 21,1940, until her death

Children: Patricia (Tricia) Nixon and Julie Nixon

Places She Lived: Ely, Nevada (1912–1913), Artesia (Cerritos), California (1913–1932), New York City (1932–1934, 1963–1969, 1980–1981), Los Angeles (1934–1937, 1961–1963), Whittier (1937–1942, 1946–1947), Washington, D.C. (1942, 1947–1961, 1969–1974), San Clemente, California (1974–1980), Park Ridge, New Jersey (1981–1993)

Major Achievements:

   ✶ Entertained a record-breaking 109,000 White House guests at formal dinners, teas, luncheons, and receptions, which often included ordinary citizens

   ✶ Arranged for nondenominational religious services to be held on Sundays in the East Room of the White House

   ✶ Oversaw the 1971 wedding of her daughter Tricia to Edward F. Cox, the first White House wedding held in the Rose Garden

   ✶ Made the White House more accessible to visitors by having the outside lit at night and by having ramps installed for people in wheelchairs

   ✶ Took an active role in encouraging Americans to become volunteers

   ✶ Became the most widely traveled First Lady by visiting 83 countries and was the first First Lady to visit Africa and the People's Republic of China

Fast Facts about
Richard Milhous Nixon's Presidency

Terms of Office: Elected in 1968 and reelected in 1972; served as the thirty-seventh president of the United States from 1969 until he resigned in 1974 because of the Watergate scandal

Vice Presidents: Spiro T. Agnew (1969–1973) and Gerald Ford (1973–1974); Agnew resigned because he was charged with committing fraud while governor of Maryland; Ford became president of the United States when Nixon resigned

Major Policy Decisions and Legislation:

* Imposed limits on increases in wages and prices of goods in order to improve the economy (1971)
* At the 1972 summit conference in Moscow, signed agreements with the Soviet Union to limit nuclear weapons
* Directed negotiations that ended American involvement in the Vietnam War and provided for the return of American prisoners of war (1973)

Major Events:

* President Nixon appoints Warren Burger chief justice of the Supreme Court (1969) and appoints three associate justices to the Supreme Court: Harry Blackmun (1970), Lewis Powell (1972), and William Rehnquist (1972).
* Demonstrations against U.S. involvement in the Vietnam War take place across the country (1969–1970).
* The Twenty-sixth Amendment is added to the Constitution (1971), allowing citizens eighteen years old and older to vote.
* Nixon opens talks with the People's Republic of China and becomes the first U.S. president to visit that country (February 1972).
* On June 17, 1972, burglars with ties to the White House break into the headquarters of the Democratic National Committee in the Watergate Complex.
* The Senate Watergate Committee hearings and the House Judiciary Committee hearings find that Nixon tried to cover up the Watergate break-in. Rather than be impeached, Nixon became the first U.S. president to resign from office.

Where to Visit

Museum of American History of the Smithsonian Institution
"First Ladies: Political and Public Image"
14th Street and Constitution Avenue, N.W.
Washington, D.C.
(202) 357-2008

Richard M. Nixon Library
Pat Nixon Room
18001 Yorba Linda Boulevard
Yorba Linda, California 92686
(714) 993-3393
(714) 993-5075

White House
1600 Pennsylvania Avenue
Washington, D.C. 20500
(202) 456-1414
Visitors Office: (202) 456-7041

National Archives
Constitution Avenue
Washington, D.C.
(202) 501-5000

The Nixon Center for Peace and Freedom
1620 I Street N.W., Suite 900
Washington, D. C.

Watergate Hotel
2650 Virginia Avenue N.W.
Washington. D.C.
(202) 965-2300

Online Sites of Interest

Chapman University
http://www.chapman.edu/nixon/
This site contains the home page for the Richard Nixon Library and Birthplace

The First Ladies of the United States of America
http://www2.whitehouse.gov/WH/glimpse/firstladies/html/firstladies.html
A portrait and biographical sketch of each First Lady plus links to other White House sites

George Magazine
http://www.georgemag.com/curissue/DecJan95/watergate/pat.html
An article containing a short bio of Pat Nixon

Grolier Online
http://gi.grolier.com/presidents/aae/inaugs/
This site includes biography, inaugural address, and quick facts about President Richard M. Nixon

History Happens
http://www.usahistory.com/presidents
A site that contains fast facts about Richard M. Nixon, including personal information, inaugural address, and term in office

Tezcat Network
http://tezcat.com/~nrn/nixon/nixon.shtml
This Nixon site includes topics such as Nixon in the News, Speeches, Digital Nixon, and other Nixon links

Virtual Elections
http://virtual election.cbc.net/37.html
A site containing information about Richard M. Nixon

The White House
http://www.whitehouse.gov/WH/Welcome.html
Information about the current president and vice president; White House history and tours; biographies of past presidents and their families; a virtual tour of the historic building, current events, and much more

The White House for Kids
http://www.whitehouse.gov/WH/kids/html/kidshome.html
Includes information about White House kids, past and present; famous "First Pets," past and present; historic moments of the presidency; and much more.

For Further Reading

Barr, Roger. *The Importance of Richard M. Nixon*. San Diego: Lucent Books, Inc., 1992.

Clinton, Susan M. *First Ladies*. Cornerstones of Freedom series. Chicago: Childrens Press, 1994.

Devaney, John. *The Vietnam War*. New York: Franklin Watts, 1992.

Fisher, Leonard E. *The White House*. New York: Holiday House, 1989.

Gormley, Beatrice. *First Ladies*. New York: Scholastic, Inc., 1997.

Gould, Lewis L. (ed.). *American First Ladies: Their Lives and Their Legacy*. New York: Garland Publishing, 1996.

Guzzetti, Paula. *The White House*. Parsippany, N. J.: Silver Burdett Press, 1995.

Kent, Deborah. *The White House*. Chicago: Childrens Press, 1994.

Kilian, Pamela. *What Was Watergate? A Young Reader's Guide to Understanding an Era*. New York: St. Martin's Press, 1990.

Klapthor, Margaret Brown. *The First Ladies*. 8th edition. Washington, D.C.: White House Historical Association, 1995.

Larsen, Rebecca. *Richard Nixon: The Rise and Fall of a President*. New York: Franklin Watts, 1991.

Lillegard, Dee. *Richard Nixon: Thirty-seventh President of the United States*. Encyclopedia of Presidents series. Chicago: Childrens Press, 1988.

Mayo, Edith P. (ed.). *The Smithsonian Book of the First Ladies: Their Lives, Times, and Issues*. New York: Henry Holt, 1996.

Sandak, Cass. *The Nixons*. New York: Crestwood House, 1992.

Index

Page numbers in **boldface type** indicate illustrations

Photo Identifications

Cover: Official White House portrait of Patricia Ryan Nixon
Page 8: Pat Ryan at the age of twelve
Page 22: Pat Ryan at work in the Old Seton Hospital pharmacy
Page 34: Richard, Pat, and Tricia Nixon in 1946, about the time Richard won a seat in the U.S. House of Representatives
Page 48: Pat and Richard with their daughters Julie and Tricia, just after Richard was nominated the Republican candidate for vice president in 1952
Page 66: Pat and Richard at daughter Tricia's wedding
Page 88: The Nixon family celebrating Pat and Richard's fiftieth wedding anniversary

Photo Credits©

About the Author

Barbara Silberdick Feinberg graduated with honors from Wellesley College where she was elected to Phi Beta Kappa. As a Wellesley summer intern in Washington, D.C., she met Pat Nixon at a reception at the Nixon home and found her to be a very warm and attractive person. Mrs. Feinberg holds a Ph.D. in political science from Yale University. Among her more recent books are *Watergate: Scandal in the White House*; *American Political Scandals Past and Present*; *The National Government*; *State Governments*; *Local Governments*; *Words in the News: A Student's Dictionary of American Government and Politics*; *Harry S. Truman*; *John Marshall: The Great Chief Justice*; *Electing the President*; *The Cabinet*; *Hiroshima and Nagasaki*; *Black Tuesday: The Stock Market Crash of 1929*; *Term Limits for Congress*; *The Constitutional Amendments*; and *Next in Line: The American Vice Presidency*. She has also written *Marx and Marxism*; *The Constitution: Yesterday, Today, and Tomorrow*; and *Franklin D. Roosevelt, Gallant President*. She is a contributor to *The Young Reader's Companion to American History*.

Mrs. Feinberg lives in New York City with her younger son Douglas and two Yorkshire terriers, Katie and Holly. Among her hobbies are growing African violets, collecting antique autographs of historical personalities, listening to the popular music of the 1920s and 1930s, and working out in exercise classes.